ALPHABETS
OLD & NEW

ALPHABETS
OLD & NEW

LEWIS F. DAY

SENATE

Alphabets Old & New

This third edition first published in 1910
by B. T. Batsford, London

This edition published in 1995 by Senate, an imprint of
Studio Editions Ltd, Princess House, 50 Eastcastle Street,
London W1N 7AP, England

ISBN 1 85958 160 9
Printed and bound in Guernsey by
The Guernsey Press Co. Ltd

PREFACE TO THE THIRD EDITION.

A BOOK of alphabets like this, for the use of artists and others who have occasion either to work in the manner of some given period or to design lettering of their own, needs scarcely any introductory essay.

I have attempted, however, in " Art in the Alphabet," to give, as simply as possible, that amount of information about the Alphabet and its evolution without which it is not safe for the designer to depart from too familiar forms.

Fuller particulars of the various alphabets than it was possible to give in this connected and condensed account of the alphabet will be found in the Descriptive List of Illustrations.

My own ideas on lettering design, enunciated by the way, are the more frankly expressed because it must be understood that they are only personal opinions which the reader will take for what they are worth.

In the alphabets themselves the spirit of the old lettering is faithfully kept, though I have not scrupled to supply missing letters. Scholars will of course object to this ; but the book is not for them ; it is for working artists, who will be glad, I know, to have twenty-six letters to the alphabet.

A feature in the book is the quantity of illustrations showing the difference it makes in the character of the lettering, whether it is in wood or stone, in stuff or leather, in mosaic or stained glass ; whether, for example in metal, it is cut in, grounded out, beaten up, onlaid or engraved ; or whether the writing tool chances to be a chisel or a gouge, a needle or a brush, a stylus or a pen—and even what sort of pen it is.

All this is much more fully illustrated than it was in earlier editions ; and, in particular, the penmanship of the 17th century for which I have been able to draw upon a unique collection of the famous " Writing Books " in the possession of the publisher.

" Alphabets Old and New " concerns itself only with letters and the corresponding numerals. The decorative use of Lettering in Ornament is the subject of a separate volume.

LEWIS F. DAY.

15, TAVITON STREET,
March 1, 1910.

TABLE OF CONTENTS.

DESCRIPTIVE LIST OF ILLUSTRATIONS.

1. GREEK ALPHABET—From a MS.—characteristic of the pen. (Compare the B with 54 and 55, and observe the likeness of the Ω to W.) 9th century.

2. COPTIC MS.—10th century or earlier. ⎫

3. COPTIC MS.—12th century. ⎬ Compare with Greek.

4. COPTIC MS.—14th century. ⎭

5. GREEK MS.—11th century.

6. ROMAN MS.—Penwork. A has no cross-stroke. Upstrokes thick and thin. (Compare 30.) 4th century.

7. MS.—Penwork. Round D and M. G has a tail. 7th century.

8. ROMAN UNCIALS—Penwork. 8th century.

9. "RUSTIC" ROMAN—Penwork. A has no cross-stroke. F and L rise above line. E, I, T not easy to read. 5th century.

10. ROMAN CAPITALS—Penwork. R has thin upstroke. 6th century.

11. ROMAN CAPITALS—Penwork. (Compare square O with 17, 18, 48.) Note "dilation" of strokes. 6th century.

12. BYZANTINE CAPITALS—7th century.

13. ENGLISH INSCRIPTION—From a monument to the sister of William the Conqueror. 1085.

14. FRANCO-GALLIC CAPITALS—Heading of a MS. Penwork, of which the curly quirks are indicative. 7th century.

15. VISIGOTHIC MS.—Moresque influence perceptible. Note long and short letters. 10th century.

68. GERMAN MS.—Initials. Distinctly penwork. Departing again widely from the square Roman form. 12th century.

69. GOTHIC UNCIALS—From the Arundel and Lansdowne MSS. in the British Museum. Written with a rather frisky pen. English. End of 12th century.

70. LETTERS apparently scraped out of a coat of varnish colour upon gilt metal—From an altar at Lisbjerg in Denmark. 12th century.

71. GOTHIC UNCIALS—From a Bible in the British Museum (15'409). Characteristically penwork. 13th century. (Compare 69.)

72. GOTHIC UNCIALS—From the inscription upon a bronze bell at Hildesheim. 1270.

73. GOTHIC UNCIALS—From a Psalter from St. Albans, now in the British Museum (2. B. VI.). Penwork. 13th century. (Compare 71.)

74. MS. LETTERS—Typically Gothic capitals. "Closed" letters. Sportive finishing strokes. 14th century.

75. ITALIAN CAPITALS—Drawn by J. Vinycomb. 14th century.

76. INCISED GOTHIC CAPITALS—From Italy, Spain, and south of France. About 1350.

77 and 78. GOTHIC INSCRIPTIONS—From Nordhausen. Cut in brass. 1395—1397.

79. ENGLISH GOTHIC INSCRIPTIONS. Stone. From monument of Richard II. in Westminster Abbey, and others of same date. About 1400.

80. ENGLISH INITIALS—From MS. in the British Museum. On a background of delicate ornament, penned in red. About 1400.

81. GOTHIC MINUSCULE—From the Church of S. Francesco at Prato. Simple forms incised in marble and filled in with cement. About 1410.

82. GOTHIC LETTERS carved in stone—The ground sunk. Spanish. 14th or 15th century. (Compare 31.)

83. PENWORK—Severe and straight beginning of a type which eventually becomes excessively flowing and florid. 1420.

lacings. But the knotting occupies approximately the
natural thickness of the letter ; and, though the outline
is thus broken, the form of the letter is sufficiently pre-
served. This splitting of the letter, as it were, into
ribbons in its thickest parts was not uncommon in 16th-
century initials. It is obvious that any form of letter
might be elaborated after this fashion. 1523.

197. MODERN GOTHIC RIBBAND ALPHABET—Engraved on brass, the ground cross-hatched. Adapted from Otto Hupp.

198. MODERN CAPITALS drawn with a continuous line, such as a silk cord "couched" upon velvet would naturally take, and suitable, therefore, for that form of embroidery. The flowing line is here as much dictated by the conditions as the square and angular forms of the letters following the mesh of the canvas in 200. This alphabet might equally well be traced with a full brush, and so executed in paint or gesso. It was worked by Mary Kidd of S. Mary's Embroidery School, Wantage.

199. MODERN CAPITALS EMBOSSED on thin sheet-metal, the form and fashion of the letters suggested by the ease with which they could be beaten up. L. F. D.

200. EMBROIDERED ALPHABET, founded upon some letters in an old English sampler—The peculiar angularity of the forms follows naturally from working on the lines given by the mesh of the canvas, and is characteristic of a certain class of very simple needlework. L. F. D. (Compare with 126 and 202, and with what is said in reference to 198.)

201. MODERN CAPITALS AND LOWER CASES—Scratched straight off in moist clay, afterwards baked. The form of the letters is such as could be most easily incised with a point or stylus, and is characteristic of the way of working out of which it comes. L. F. D. (Compare with 198, 191, 192.)

202. MODERN ALPHABET IN RIGHT LINES, suggested by the square form of Chinese writing. L. F. D. (See p. 29. Compare with 200.)

203. MODERN ALPHABET, expressive of the brush, suggested by brush forms in Japanese writing. L. F. D. (See p. 29.)

204. MODERN BRUSHWORK LETTERS after Mucha.

205. MODERN STENCILLED ALPHABET adapted from E. Grasset and M. P. Verneuil.

249. VARIOUS DATES—1573, Flemish, engraved on steel. 1747, German, twisted brass wire inlaid in wood.

250. FANCIFUL NUMERALS. L. F. D.

251. MODERN.

252. MODERN—L. F. D. (Compare with 191, 192, 198.)

253. MODERN GERMAN—Alois Müller.

254. MODERN—L. F. D. (Compare with 217.)

NOTE.—Other numerals occur in illustrations—

142.	A.D. 1665.	
143.	A.D. 1697.	
155.	MODERN.	Caslon type.
169.	,,	J. W. Weekes.
170.	,,	Bailey Scott Murphy.
171 and 172.	,,	R. Anning Bell.
173.	,,	A. Beresford Pite.
176.	,,	Percy Smith.
189.	,,	Type.
211.	,,	J. Cromar Watt.
218.	,,	Patten Wilson.

ART IN THE ALPHABET.

THERE are two conditions on which the artist may be permitted to tamper with the alphabet : whatever he does ought, in the first place, to make reading run smoother, and, in the second, to make writing satisfactory to the eye. Neither of these desirable ends should, however, be sought at the expense of the other.

The way to make reading easier is to mark whatever is characteristic in the letter ; to develop what is peculiar to it ; to curtail, or it may be to lop off, anything which tends to make us confound it with another ; to emphasize, in short, the individuality of each individual letter, and make it unmistakable. At the same time, there is no reason why reading should not be made pleasant as well as easy. Beauty, that is to say, is worth bearing in mind. It must not, of course, interfere with use ; but there is not the least reason why it should. Beauty does not imply elaboration or ornament. On the contrary, simplicity and character, and the dignity which comes of them, are demanded in the interests alike of practicality and of art.

It is impossible judiciously to modify the letters of the alphabet as it is, or as at any given time it was, without thoroughly understanding how it came to be so. The form and feature of lettering are explained only by its descent.

All writing is a sort of shorthand. It is inevitable that the signs used to represent sounds should be reduced to their simplest expression. They become in the end mere signs, as unlike the thing which may have suggested them in the first instance as a man's signature, which is yet honoured by his banker, is unlike his name : enough if writing convey what we are meant to understand : the business of a letter is to symbolize a definite sound.

We arrive, then, by a process of what has been termed " degradation " of such natural forms as were first employed in picture-writing (call it rather adaptation), at an alphabet of seemingly arbitrary signs, the alphabet as we know it after a couple of thousand years and more. So well do we know it that we seldom think to ask ourselves what the letters mean, or how they came to be.

The explanation of these forms lies in their evolution.

Our alphabet is that of the Romans. We speak of it to this day as Roman, to distinguish it from Gothic or black letter. The Romans had it from the Greeks, or, if not immediately from them, from the same sources whence they drew theirs.

Certainly the Greek, Etruscan, and old Roman

alphabets were all very much alike. They resembled one another in the number of letters they contained, in the sound-value of those letters, and in the form they took. There were sixteen letters common to Greeks and Etruscans: ΑΒΓΔΕΙΚΛΜ ΝΟΠΡΣΤΥ; and this number sufficed always for

ΑΔΒΒΒΓΔΕЄЄЄŹΖ

ΗΘΦΙΚΚΛΜⱣΜΝΟ

ΟΠℲℲΡΤΥΥΦΧΧΨШ

I. GREEK MS. 9TH CENTURY.

the Etruscans, the race dying out before ever it had need of more. The Greeks had no longer (as the Egyptians had) any signs to represent syllables, that is to say combinations of vowels and consonants. They added to the alphabet, which they borrowed, with modifications, from the Phœnicians, extra letters to express words of their own. The Greek ΥΦΧΨΩ do not occur in

Ⲉⲱⲱⲡⲧⲉⲗⲉⲟ
ⲉⲣⲱⲁⲛⲅⲉⲛ
ⲙⲏⲛⲱⲉⲡ
ⲙⲧⲟⲓ ⲏⲛ
ⲁⲛⲟⲩⲣⲱⲉ
ⲕⲱⲧⲉⲉⲩⲡⲟ
ⲗⲓⲥⲉⲣⲟⲉⲓⲥ
ⲉⲣⲟⲥ

2. COPTIC MS. 5TH TO 10TH CENTURY.

the Phœnician alphabet. The Phœnicians had
probably adopted from the Egyptians signs to
express foreign sounds new to their own language,
without knowing or caring anything about the
pictorial origin of such signs. There was thus no
reason why they should not modify what they
regarded as arbitrary expressions of sound-values,
and every reason why they should reduce them to
the very simplest and most conveniently written
shape—which they did ; and so it comes about that
we to-day are in all probability directly indebted to
ancient Egypt for at least a portion of our alphabet,
far removed as it may be from the hieroglyphics
of the Pharaohs   That, however, is by the way,

and, besides, a long way off. For present purposes
we need not go further back than to ancient
Greece.

The Romans dropped all compound consonants, using at first the two consonants which
most nearly expressed the sound equivalent to
that of the Greek double letter; for example, PH
in place of Φ. But they proceeded also to devise
single letters for sounds which until then had
been expressed by two; F, for example, instead
of PH.

A Greek alphabet of the year 394 B.C. is given
in illustration 54, and a 16th-century version in 55.

3. COPTIC MS. 12TH CENTURY.

4. COPTIC MS. 14TH CENTURY.

The more cursive form employed by the 9th-century scribe is shown in the manuscript letters (1) on page 3, whilst the more careful and elaborate writing proper to gold letters is illustrated by a page of 11th-century work (5) from a MS. in the Laurentian Library at Florence.

It is interesting to compare with these the Coptic writing (2, 3, 4), which is obviously only a variant upon the Greek; for the Christianized Egyptians, when they accepted Christianity, adopted the Greek alphabet, just as the Turks took the Arabic character at the time they accepted the Koran; and when, in the 6th century, the new faith was firmly established at Alexandria, Coptic writing supplanted the old Egyptian. So it happens that the Coptic alphabet is Greek, except for seven extra signs, taken from the ancient demotic alphabet, to express Egyptian sounds for which the Greeks had no equivalent.

The early Roman or Latin alphabet differed very little from the Greek. The latest comers in it were G H K Q X Y Z.

In its adaptation to the Latin language, Greek gamma or G becomes C. G is, in fact, almost equivalent to *hard* C. To the not too subtle ear the two sounds are like enough to pass one for the other, just as *soft* C may be made to do duty for S. When G came to be used as a separate letter, distinct from C, then C in its turn was used for K, though K did not go quite out of use.

5. GREEK MS.　IITH CENTURY.

The letter J did not exist either in the Greek or in the ancient Roman alphabet. It is equivalent to II. Place one I over the other and you get a long $\frac{I}{I}$. Eventually the initial developed a tail, and became J. Towards the 15th century the initial I was pretty generally written J.

The Greek Υ (*upsilon*) becomes the Roman Y. The letters U and V were long considered as interchangeable; one or other of them might be used, or both at once in the same word in the same sense. It was not until the 10th century that the custom arose of using V before a vowel, and else-where using U.

Though Ω (*omega*) stood for long O, the Latin letter, which was derived in form from it, bore the value of W. And, as may be seen in the 9th-century alphabet on page 3, omega was sometimes *written* precisely like a W.

The alphabet, as we know it, owes something also to Scandinavia. The Runic writing, as the script of the Scandinavian and other Northern European priesthood was called, dates back to legendary days. It was the invention, they say, of Odin himself. If so, Odin, to judge by internal evidence, must have derived it from some earlier Greek or Roman source. What we know is, that it was in use from the time of the first intercourse between Scandinavians and Romans. The Christian Church forbade its use, and with the triumph

ABCDEFGHILM
NOPQRSTUY

6. ROMAN MS. 4TH CENTURY.

of Christianity it passed out of currency; but it
lived long enough to affect in some degree our
Anglo-Saxon writing.

It will be well now to mark the more decided
steps in the progress of the alphabet. The type
we use takes, as every one knows, two forms—a
larger and a smaller, a major and a minor, or, as
printers put it, " capitals " and " lower case," or
the small letters which, being most continually in
request, it is convenient to keep near at hand, in
the lower part of the case, from which the com-
positor, so to speak, feeds himself. Our written
character takes the form of a " running " hand,
and is known by that name, or by the more
high-sounding title of " cursive."

ABCDEFGHILM
NOPQRSTUWXZ

7. MS. 7TH CENTURY.

ABCDEFGHIKLM
NOPQRSTUVY

8. ROMAN UNCIALS. 8TH CENTURY.

Now, the printer's "lower case," or "minuscule," as it is also called, is practically the book form of running hand, except that the letters are quite separate, not conjoined as they are in what pretends to be only the hand of the ready writer, and does not claim to be beautiful at all.

The earlier form, whether of Greek or Roman letter, was the capital, the square shape, with relatively few curved lines, which could conveniently be cut in stone or engraved on metal. This is, in fact, the *monumental* style—adapted to, and, what is more, inspired by, the chisel or the

ABCDEFGHILM
NOPQRSTVY

9. ROMAN "RUSTIC" WRITING. 5TH CENTURY.

ABCDEFGHILM

NOPQRSTVY

10. ROMAN MS. CAPITALS. 6TH CENTURY.

graver.   You have only to look at it (54, 56, 57) to see how precisely fit it is for its purpose.   There is no mistake about it, it is incision.

Manuscript writers adopted for book writing a different character, or rather they adapted the square capital letter to more ready execution with the pen, and so evolved a rounder kind of letter which is known by the name of *uncial*—not that it was invariably inch-long, as the term is supposed to imply.

The uncial form of writing is intermediate, you will see (8), between the monumental writing and the " current " hand of the ready writer.   It is, if not the step between the two, a compromise between them—no matter which ; what it concerns us to know is that calligraphy took that direction, which goes to explain many a later form of letter widely differing from the original square type.   The relationship between these uncial letters and the cursive Greek (1) is obvious.

The uncial character does not so much affect the modern printer ; but it is the form of letter from

AAACDEFILM
OOPORSTV

II. MS. CAPITALS. 6TH CENTURY.

which the artist who prefers his own handiwork to that of the printing press has perhaps most to learn.

A squarer form of capital employed by the Romans in manuscripts of the 5th and two following centuries, is known by the name of "rustic"; not that there was anything rustic about these capitals in our sense of the word; but the Latin word was used in the sense of free and easy, *sans gêne*. The character of the writing is not so formal as was supposed to befit the town. It is a kind of country cousin; it stands, let us say, for the Roman capital in a loose coat and a soft hat. The characteristic points about it (9) are that the vertical strokes are all very thin, and the cross-strokes broad. These cross-strokes take the form of a kind of tick, tapering at the ends; and similar ticks are used to emphasize the finishing of the thin strokes. That all of this is pen-work is self-evident. But, as before said, the more usual form of penmanship at that time was the uncial letter.

ABCDEFGHIK
LNOPRSTVX

12. BYZANTINE CAPITALS. 7TH CENTURY.

Even when the Roman manuscript writers used, as they sometimes did, the square capital form, they did not confine themselves (11) to the severely simple shapes which came naturally to the lapidaries. The unequal strength of the lines, the thickening of the strokes at the ends, and the spurred or forked shapes they take, all speak of the pen; not the steel pen, of course, nor yet the more supple quill, but the reed pen—rather blunter than a quill, but pliant enough, and not given to spluttering. Moreover, it did not tempt the writer to indulge in unduly thin upstrokes.

Capitals, Greek and Roman alike, represent, roughly speaking, the first accepted shapes, engraver's or carver's work. Uncials stand for MS. writing, scribe's work, growing by degrees rounder and more current. The smaller minuscule was evolved out of the running hand of the mercantile, as distinguished from the literary, scribe. It was not used by the ancient Romans, and it was not until towards the 8th century that running hand was thus reduced to, order. The greater part of what is called cursive writing scarcely concerns

ABCDEFGMN
OPQRSTVX

13. INSCRIPTION CUT IN STONE. A.D. 1085.

the calligrapher; it might equally be called discursive, so apt is it to run wild, in which case it tells less of the progress of writing than of the caprice or carelessness of the individual writer.

That was not the case with the various ceremonial versions of running hand employed by the writers of Papal Bulls and Royal Charters. Such "diplomatic" hands, as they are styled (because diplomas were written in them), and the so-called "Chancery" hands, are highly elaborate, and in a sense ornamental, but they are so unlike our writing as to be, practically speaking, illegible. They are very suggestive for all that. A specimen of English Court hand is given in Alphabet 157.

With the decline of the Roman empire came naturally the demoralization of the Roman character, capital or uncial; and just in proportion as Rome ceased to be the one centre of the world, and other nations rose into importance, so their writing began to show signs of nationality. At the loss of some refinement, we get thenceforth variety of character. By the beginning of the 8th century distinctly national styles of lettering were evolved.

To subdivide these styles so minutely as the learned do, is rather to bewilder the poor student by their multitude. The important European races were the Latins, the Franks, the Teutons, and Anglo-Saxons, and the Visigoths; and from them we get respectively the Lombard, the Frankish,

14. FRANCO-GALLIC MSS. HEADLINES. 7TH CENTURY.

the Teutonic and Anglo-Saxon, and the Visigothic types of writing, all of which eventually merge themselves in what we call Gothic, in which, nevertheless, we still find traits of nationality, English, French, Italian, German, Spanish, as the case may be.

First as to the Lombardic character, which prevailed in Italy from the 8th to the 11th century. It was not, as its name might be taken to imply, the invention of the Lombards. They were just long-bearded conquerors, and invented nothing. The character was not even confined to Northern

Italy; only it happened first to be developed there, and so all later Latin writing (after the Empire) came to be called "Lombardic."

It has already been explained how uncial writing was transitional between square "caps" and rounder pen-forms. The Lombardic shows a further stage of transition. The penman had not quite made up his mind between straight lines and curved; he hesitated between the square-lined M and N and the rounded forms (19, 20, 68). Eventually he decided in favour of the bulging shapes, which in their later development we distinguish by the name of Lombardic capitals (74).

There is a broken-backed version of the Lombard minuscule, "*Lombard brisée*" the French call it, which, though not intrinsically beautiful, is interesting as foreshadowing the later form of Gothic "lower case" which we call "black letter."

Our own "lower case" we get more or less directly from Charlemagne. He found, perhaps his friend the Pope told him, that writing had degenerated by the time he came to the throne (A.D. 800) to a state unworthy of a mighty emperor. Accordingly he ordained its reformation. He went so far as to compel bishops and other important personages who could not write decently to employ scribes who could. In this way he revived the small Roman character, which we eventually adopted for our printed type.

The scribes of Charlemagne (and for some time

after him) did not yet manage to fashion very
satisfactory capitals.   They still mixed up letters
all of one thickness with others in which thick and
thin strokes, or diminishing strokes, were used in a
most illogical and awkward way (64)—indicative, of
course, of a period of change.   But they did arrive
at a satisfactory and very characteristic rendering

INIE DNI INEPT OPSELM
PREFATIONSINQVA
EXPRIMITVR HVMILIS

15. VISIGOTHIC MS.   IOTH CENTURY.

of minuscule lettering.   A conspicuous feature in
it was the elongation of the longer limb of the
l p g q f d—*tails*, that is to say, came into fashion,
and long ones, as much as four or five times the
length of the body of the letter.   The letter s took
also the long form, ſ.   The letter t, on the other
hand, does not rise much above the line, sometimes
not at all.

16. SAXON ILLUMINATION (CAROLINE). 9TH CENTURY.

That elongation of up-and-down strokes is characteristic of Frankish and Visigothic lettering generally. It occurs even in the case of capitals, as in the headlines of the 10th-century MS. on p. 18. There the I, the H, and the L rise high above the heads of their fellows, whilst, on the other hand, the V-shaped U in the word OPVSCVLVM is reduced to more than modest proportions.

There appears to be in Visigothic lettering, of which that is a good example, usually a trace of Moorish influence, betraying itself in the liberties taken with the *proportion* of the characters; the Moors had by that time overrun Spain.

17. ANGLO-SAXON.

ᚪⴱcⴷⴹϝᵹⴸⱈʝⱞ ⱡ·ⴗoⴖⴳᵹꞅⱦⱦⱵ

18. ANGLO-SAXON MS. 9TH CENTURY.

There is something very whimsical about the character of Anglo-Saxon capitals ; at times mechanically square in form, at others exceptionally flowing and even frisky (16, 17, 62, 63). Anglo-Saxon lettering was affected by lingering traces of an obsolete alphabet derived perhaps at some remote period from the Gauls, which, to judge by internal evidence, must have been something like the Greek.   In the minuscule character (18) there is a curious twist in the long stroke of the b and l.

By the 13th century the Gothic style had formed itself.   In the next hundred years or more it was perfected.   At the end of the 15th century it was

AᴄDEEEILMNNOPQ

QRSTUV

19. FLORENTINE, INCISED AND INLAID. 12TH CENTURY.

still flourishing—flourishing was the word literally
—in the 16th letters were sometimes nearly all
flourish : it takes an expert to read them.

The Gothic variations upon the Roman capital
form are characteristic : the thick strokes are not
even-sided, but expanded at the two ends or
narrowed towards the centre ; the curved strokes
do not swell so gradually as before, but bulge

ALDDOEHL
IMNDOPRSY

20. ITALIAN MS. EARLY 13TH CENTURY.

more or less suddenly ; the tails of sundry letters
break insubordinate from the ranks ; and the ex-
tremities are often foliated or otherwise orna-
mented (66, 69, 71). Markedly characteristic of
Gothic of the 13th and 14th centuries are also
the " closed " letters, of which examples occur in
Alphabets 76, 77, 78, 80, etc.

What are called Lombardic capitals were used,
not only as initials, but for inscriptions throughout.
In fact, it was not until the 15th century that

inscriptions were commonly written in minuscule letters. In many cases these Lombard capitals were not written with a pen, but with a brush, from which results something of their character. The brush lines were fatter than pen strokes.

Gothic characteristics, however, only gradually

ABCDEFGHI JKLMNOPQR STUVWXYZ

21. FREE RENDERING OF LOMBARD MSS. ABOUT 1250.

asserted themselves, and individual scribes clung tenaciously to the older forms. The alphabet opposite, for example, though of the 15th century, only mildly represents the period to which by date it belongs.

Gothic letters lend themselves to more variety in design than Roman, not being so perfect in themselves. To some, perhaps, they are more interesting on that very account: perfection palls upon us. Anyway, the Gothic forms are often very beautiful. The Roman letter is classic, and therefore fixed—or, should it rather be said, it is fixed, and therefore classic?

With regard to the Gothic minuscule character (23, 24, 25), the even perpendicularity of the broad, straight strokes gives at a glance the character distinguished as " black letter," because it is rela-

ABCDEFGHIILM NOPORSTVXZ

22. CAPITALS. 15TH CENTURY.

tively much heavier than the Roman minuscule. You have only to compare the two to see that the " black letter " *is* blacker.

The Germans marked this form of lettering for their own, and persevered in its use long after the rest of the world, in pursuance of the fashion of classicism prevailing in the 16th century, had abandoned it for the Roman style of lettering.

The mediæval German version of black letter was stronger than that of other countries, the French more fanciful, the Italian more refined, more perfect, but perhaps never so Gothic.

The old " black letter " varied, as will be seen,

abcdefghi
klmnopqrʒ
ſstůvwxyʒ

23. GERMAN GOTHIC MINUSCULE.

very much in character. The rounder form (23) is freer, easier to write, more cursive. The more regular and straight-backed letter (24, 25) went rather out of fashion for a while; but it was revived by the printers, who saw in it what they could best imitate.

The type we use nowadays has shaped itself in a more or less accidental way. In the first place, it was a copy of manuscript forms. That was inevitable. Possibly printers were anxious to palm off their printed books as manuscripts. But, apart from any such intent on their part, their text was bound to follow the written page, or no one would have been able to read it. And as, at the time of

abcdefghi
klmnopqr
ꝛsctuvryz

24. GERMAN GOTHIC MINUSCULE.

the introduction of printing, two styles of writing were in use for manuscripts, there arose naturally two styles of printed type—" Roman " and " black letter." In printing, as in manuscript, however, black letter gave way to the Roman character, but not all at once ; there was a period of transition during which some very interesting and characteristic types were used. We in our day have arrived, by a process of copying the copies of copies of copies, from which all the virtue of vitality and freshness has died out, at a 20th century type (look at the newspapers), which compares most unfavourably with the early printing.   The modern form of letter is in a measure fixed for us by

abcdefghi

klmnopqrs

stuvůwxyz

25. GOTHIC MINUSCULE.

circumstances; we cannot conveniently depart far
from it ; but something may be done.   There is
no need to revive mediæval lettering, no occasion
to invent new lettering all out of our own heads, if
that were possible ; any new departure of ours
must be very much on old lines ; but at least we
might found ourselves upon the best that has been
done, and go straight to that for inspiration.

Type, as before said, was based on manuscript
forms.   These manuscript forms had been shaped
with a view always to easy writing.   What was
difficult to pen dropped out of use, and lettering
became what the scribe made it.   The considera-
tions, however, which guided the writer no longer
concern the printer.   It is time, perhaps, he took
stock of the alphabet—looked over it with a view

to its perfection, since one shape is about as easy to *print* as another. The changes which have taken place in our printed type during the last three hundred years or so may very likely have been on the whole in the direction of easy reading, but they have not been in the direction of beauty ; and it is quite likely that it may be worth while restoring some obsolete forms of letter now that we have not to write them. There is inconvenience in departing in any appreciable degree from the accepted form of letter ; but we have arrived to-day at a period when everyone is so familiar with the printed page that, prejudiced as we may be against any modification of it, there is no danger of our finding any real difficulty in reading an improved type. Lettering is none the more legible because it is ugly : beauty is compatible with the very sternest use.

The earliest writing was most probably scratched with a point upon whatever came handiest to the scribe—skins, palm leaves, or the bark of trees, and especially upon clay, a material which had only to be burnt to become more lasting than stone.

If, in scratching upon firm clay, the writer begins his stroke with a dig and then drags out the tool, it results in a wedge-shaped scratch. That seems to be the way the cuneiform character came about ; but the lettering upon the early Babylonian "bricks," as they are called, is so precisely defined that it must have been done with a sharp graver-

like point. These " wedge-shaped " or "arrow-
headed " characters came to be copied, as we know,
in stone, in which again they were about the simplest thing to cut. Three, or at most four, direct
cuts give the Ninevite character, as we know it in
the famous bas-reliefs. It is descended from clay
forms, but its own mother was the stone out of which
it was cut. The chisel was its father. Even in
inscriptions as late as the 18th century or there-
abouts, the stone-cutter lapses, as may be seen
opposite, into more or less wedge-shaped incisions ;
the chisel tempted him, and he yielded to its
persuasion.

From the cuneiform character to simple Greek
(54) or Roman (56) capitals, as square as well
could be, is not far ; and the clear-cut inscriptions
on classic monuments are still typically chisel
work. Very early Greek inscriptions are, however,
not much more than scratched in the granite or
whatever it may be. The small Greek character
on the famed Rosetta stone is *mere* scratching.

Writing done with a stylus on tablets of wax was
naturally blunt. Penwork at first was also much
blunter than modern writing—owing partly, no
doubt, to the use of the reed pen, partly to the
texture of papyrus, and partly to the consistency of
the ink. The strokes of early lettering in Egyptian,
Greek, and Latin manuscripts alike, are rather thick,
and rounded at the angles, not sharply turned.

It was a reed pen with which the Arabs wrote,

holding it more or less horizontally so as to retain
the ink, and sloping the paper or papyrus at a
convenient angle; and it was in writing the Roman
letters with a reed pen that the mediæval scribes
gave it its Gothic character. It was not until the
quill (which held the ink better) came into use that
the Italians developed their minuscule letter with
its thick and thin strokes.

A glance is sometimes enough to tell whether an
early Egyptian manuscript was written with a pen

26. FROM INSCRIPTIONS CUT IN STONE. ABOUT 1700.

or with a brush. The Arab penmen, who took
great pride in their art, wrote with a wonderfully
elastic pen, and got out of the reed forms which
remind one at times of brushwork; but the *neskhi*
character is as obviously the pen form of writing
as the squarer *cufic* is the monumental. So also we
find among the Chinese and Japanese one form of
lettering which is characteristically brushwork, and
another almost rectangular, which last is clearly
the monumental manner.

Even in late Gothic lettering we find a minuscule which is of the pen (23), and another (24, 25)
which is monumental, adapted, that is to say, to
precise and characteristic rendering with the graver
upon sheets of brass. It is curious that out of this
severe form of writing the florid ribbon character
(108) should have been evolved. But when once
the engraver began to consider the broad strokes of
his letters as bands or straps, which, by a cut of
the graver, could be made to turn over at the ends,
as indicated in Alphabet 125, it was inevitable
that a taste for the florid should lead him to
something of the kind. The wielder of the brush
was in all times induced by his implement to make
flourishes (32, 33), in which the carver had much
less temptation to indulge. The sloping or "italic"
letter (27) is, on the face of it, the product of the pen.

We find, then, that the implement employed,
stylus, reed-pen, brush, or whatever it may have
been, goes far to account for the character of
ancient lettering. So soon as the writer ceased
to be satisfied with mere scratching or blunt
indentation, and took to the use of the chisel, he
felt the need of a square cross-cut to end the
stroke of his letter. If that was broad, there was
no occasion for the cut to go beyond the width of
the stroke itself. If it was narrow, the easier
thing to do was to anticipate the danger of over-
shooting the mark, and frankly extend the end
cut. This method of finishing off the broad line

by a projecting cross-line is technically called truncation, though literally that only means cutting off. Slight but appreciable difference in character results from the angle at which the strokes are truncated or cut off.

In working with a pen, this difficulty of ending the stroke occurs only in the case of very bold lettering. In small writing the strokes naturally

a b c d e f g h
i k l m n o p q
r ſ s t u x y z

27. ROMAN ITALICS.

take pen-shape. They start square and gradually diminish, or *vice versâ*, or they thicken in the middle, according to the angle at which the pen is held, and to the pressure, which it is difficult to keep quite equal from end to end of the stroke.

It should be observed that the pressure is not naturally in the middle of the stroke, but at one end; the penman does not naturally get the symmetrical Roman O, but the Gothic O (117).

That is the pen-born shape. The even-sided O
was, if not easier to cut in stone, at least as easy ;
there was nothing to prevent symmetry, which
was accordingly the rule in sculpture. It is rather
futile to aim at that kind of thing with a pen ;
much better let the pen have its way ; and its way
is otherwise (176, 179). We get so much more out
of our tools by going with them, that it is rather
stupid to strive against them.

In very bold writing, even with a pen, the
necessity for truncating the thick strokes occurs.
You cannot easily, with one stroke of the pen,
make a thick line which begins and ends square.
It wants trimming ; and the easiest way to trim
it is by means of a fine cross-stroke extending
beyond its width. This cross-stroke T helps to
preserve and to accentuate the regularity of the
line of lettering, for which a writer worth the name
naturally has a care. The broad stroke being
rather loaded with ink, the fine cross-stroke is
inclined, in crossing it, to drag a little of the ink
with it, rounding one angle of it. The obvious
way of rectifying that is to round the opposite
angle also—and so we have the familiar finish T,
which is equivalent to the " spur " of the chiseller
mentioned just now (208).

The angle at which the cross-line joins the
stroke may be softened until it disappears, and
the stroke appears to be curved on either side—
" dilates," to use another accepted term, at the

28. ROMAN MOSAIC. LOUVRE, PARIS.

ΑΕΚΝΓΣΡΩ

29. ENGRAVED BRONZE TABLETS. NAPLES MUSEUM.

ABCDEGMNO

30. ENGRAVED BRONZE TABLETS. NAPLES MUSEUM.

31. STONE. CORDOVA. 1409.

32. PAINTED ON HISPANO-MORESQUE POTTERY.
15TH AND 16TH CENTURIES.

33. PAINTED ON ITALIAN MAJOLICA. 16TH CENTURY.

ends. Historically, we arrive at that in Lombardic and other writing as early as the 8th century (60).

Anticipating this dilation, the penman eventually made strokes in which the elementary straight line altogether disappears (68). Further elaborating, he arrived at the rather sudden swelling of the curved back of the letter, familiar in work of the 13th century and later (73, 87). With the forking of the terminations, and the breaking of the outline in various ways (20), we arrive at fantastic variation to which there is no conceivable end (34, 84, 88, 91, 120). Few instances, therefore, of the elaborate ornamentation of the lettering are here given (109, 120, 151, 152). Enough to give alphabets in which the ornamental design is in the construction of the letters themselves.

With the use of thick and thin strokes comes a difficulty. Which shall be thick, and which thin? The scribes were a long while making up their minds on that point, and they contrived some very awkward combinations (64). The solution we have at last come to is probably the best that could be found. We need scarcely bother ourselves about trying to improve upon modern practice in that respect ; it has been a case of the survival of the fittest.

Out of the use of thick and thin strokes arises the necessity for graduated strokes, there being no other way of treating the *curved* lines intermediate between the two. Then, if the thick strokes are

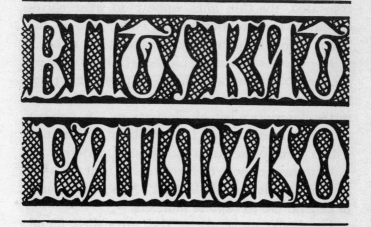

34. ENGRAVED ON BRASS. 1395.

STYGEZ CLLUTIA

35. PAINTED ON WOOD. 1727.

GNGRGY

36. PAINTED ON MAJOLICA. 1518.

truncated, the thin lines appear to want corresponding accentuation at the ends ; and so the
"serif" runs all through the alphabet (118,119, etc.).

The further influence of the writing tool upon
the form of the letter is shown on pages 32, 33, 37,
etc., and in Alphabets to which reference is made
in the descriptive list of illustrations. A number
of these Alphabets have been deliberately designed
with a view to execution in a specific material.

With regard, now, to Numerals. Until the 15th
century, the letters M, D, C, L, X, V, and I were
in general use to express numbers.

The Arabic numerals, as they are called, found
their way into Europe some time during the 12th
century, but did not come into general use before
the 15th, nor indeed much before the introduction
of printing, which diffused the knowledge of them.
Their adoption in England was more tardy than
on the continent, the beginning of the 17th century
being given as the date of their universal acceptance
here. The numerals, as we know them, or even
as they were written in the 15th century, do not
bear any marked resemblance to the genuine
Arabic ; numbers 1 and 9, and the all-important
cypher, 0, are the only Eastern figures which seem
to claim direct oriental ancestry.

The figures of the 15th century are not always
at first sight very easily legible ; the 7, for example
(227), presents anything but a familiar appearance,
but upon examination that inverted V proves to be

PTARVM

GLOSKN

37. GOLD LETTERS PICKED OUT OF BLACK PAINT. SPANISH.

AEGRS₃

38. PAINTED ON WOOD. ITALIAN. 15TH CENTURY.

AELOPQ
RSTVY

39. PAINTED ON GLAZED EARTHENWARE. ENGLISH.
18TH CENTURY.

really an equal-limbed 7 placed (as it would
naturally fall) so as to rest upon its two ends : it
is not the figure that is changed, but its position.
Much more puzzling is the early form of 4 (227,
228, 229), a loop with crossed ends upon which it
stands.   The popular explanation of the figure as
" half an eight," is anything but convincing; and it
appears to have no Eastern prototype.   There is a
17th-century version of it, however, in the Francis-
kaner Kirche, at Rothenburg (242), which, had it
been of earlier date, might have been accepted as
a satisfactory explanation.   There the loop has a
square end, and the figure rests, not upon its two
loose ends, but partly on its point.   Imagine this
figure standing upright, one point facing the left,
and it is seen to be a 4 of quite ordinary shape.   This
may not be the genesis of the form ; but, if not, it is
ingeniously imagined by the 17th-century mason.

Writers have from the first made use of contrac-
tions, the ready writer in order to save time and
trouble, the caligrapher, sculptor, and artist
generally, in order to perfect the appearance of
his handiwork, and, in many cases, to make it fit
the space with which he has to deal.   The ends of
art are not satisfied by merely compressing the
letters, or reducing them to a scale which will
enable the writer to bring them all into a given
line (208).   We, in our disregard of all but what
we call practicality, have abandoned the practice
of contraction, except in the case of diphthongs, and

BRUSH

PAINT

40. PAINTED, GERMAN GOTHIC, INITIALS.

41. COPPER RIVETS ON LEATHER. SALZBURG MUSEUM.

42. ENGRAVED IN BRASS. BRUGES.

in the exceptional instance of the word " et." The
" amperzand," as the printer calls it (225, 226), still
lingers in his founts of type, and is used even more
habitually by the ordinary penman of to-day.

To what does all this investigation of the
alphabet lead ?   It is of no use trying to evolve
brand-new alphabets out of our inner conscious-
ness.   No one would understand us, and we want
to be read.   Originality is what we all desire ; but
it is scarcely the thing to seek consciously, least of
all in lettering ; it comes of its own accord if ever
it comes.   We are original or we are not.

While the alphabet is alive there will be changes
in it, but they must inevitably be gradual ; we can
only creep on to new forms.   Practically, what we
have to do is to take an alphabet and modify it
according to our wants or inclinations, without, as
a rule, interfering much with its legibility.   A man
may, if he knows what he is about, make it more
legible, as well as in other ways bettering it.   But
to do that intelligently, he should know something
of the descent of the lettering on which he founds
himself.   That is why it has been thought worth
while to discuss the subject at such length here.

An important consideration in the design of an
alphabet—if design be not too pretentious a word
to use in speaking of what can scarcely be much
more than a variation upon orthodox forms—is
that the letters should be systematically treated.

43. APPLIED LETTERS. SILVER.

44. CARVED IN STONE. FROM BISHOP WEST'S CHAPEL, ELY
CATHEDRAL. CA. 1534.

They are more likely to be all of one family if we derive them from one source. But there is no reason why we should not cross the breed in lettering, if thereby we can improve the stock. An alphabet, however, should not *look* hybrid. The artist is free to do what he can ; but the test of success is that his creation should look as if it must be so, and could not have been otherwise.

Why, it is asked, should any one trouble himself about hand-drawn lettering, when he has ready to his use type, which is so much truer and more perfect ? Truer, perhaps, it may be, in the sense of being more mathematically exact, but it is not necessarily so truly uniform in effect ; for the unyielding letters of the type-founder come together as best they may, and if they come awkwardly he can't help it. The writer can, and indeed he should.

There is no denying that many an artist who ventures to introduce lettering into his design, does it ill, does it so carelessly, or is so easily satisfied with very indifferent penmanship, that of the two evils hard and fast letterpress would have been the lesser. None the less true is it that an artist who has been at the pains to learn to write, can, if he aim at what pen or brush will do, and refrain from entering into foolish and ineffectual rivalry with the printing press, do what that cannot do, and do better.

Looking at an early printed book, you are

45. LEAD GLAZING. AFTER WINSTON.

46. CUT LEATHER FROM A BOOK BINDING. HAMBURG MUSEUM.

47. CARVED IN STONE. ST. MARGARET'S CHURCH, KING'S LYNN. 1622.

astonished, each time afresh, at the beauty of the page. But if you go from that straight to a fine manuscript, you realize that, after all, printing, even such printing as was done by the great printers, is a makeshift. It is a makeshift we have to put up with, and we may as well make the best of it ; merely petulant complaint is childish ; but when occasion does occur, let us have the real thing, and don't let us be persuaded by readers so greedy of print as to have lost all appetite for beautiful writing, that there is no flavour or artistic savour in it. It is not good manuscript, but their spoilt palate, which is at fault.

Having perfected machinery, we are doing our best to make ourselves into machines. Until that happens—which God forbid !—man's hand is still the best, in art at all events ; and were it not the best, it would still have the charm of character, that individual quality for which a public brought up exclusively on printed type has no relish. Print, with its mechanical smoothness, and precision, has gone far to distort the modern ideal of lettering, just as photography, with its literalness, has degraded the ideal of art. There are people who resent as a sort of impertinence anything in lettering which the printing press cannot do. They are ready to take offence at whatever is unfamiliar. Really the impertinence is in a makeshift thing like type usurping any kind of authority in a matter quite beyond its scope.

48. PAINTED ON GLASS.   AFTER WINSTON.

49. ENGRAVED ON SILVER.   FROM A CUP.

50. EMBROIDERED IN GOLD THREAD.   JAMES 1ST.

51. CUT IN MARBLE. ON AN ANTIQUE BUST OF ARISTOPHANES
IN THE UFFIZI, FLORENCE.

52. STAINED AND PAINTED GLASS. FROM WINCHESTER
CATHEDRAL. AFTER WINSTON.

The great difference between old lettering and new is that in days before type-founding the scribe was free to play variations on the well-known alphabetical air, whereas our print is monotonous as the tune of a barrel organ.

53. CUT OUT OF GLAZED TILES EMBEDDED IN CEMENT. CORDOVA.

Pedants are never happy until everything is fixed. But nothing is fixed until it is dead. Life is in movement. Philosophy has long since given up the search for perpetual motion, but that is the secret of it—life; and that is the evidence and sign of life—motion. English will be a dead language when there is no longer any possibility of change in the way it is written.

OLD ALPHABETS

ARRANGED IN ORDER OF
THEIR DATE. MANY OF THEM
DIRECTLY DUE TO THE USE
OF CHISEL, PEN, BRUSH, &c.

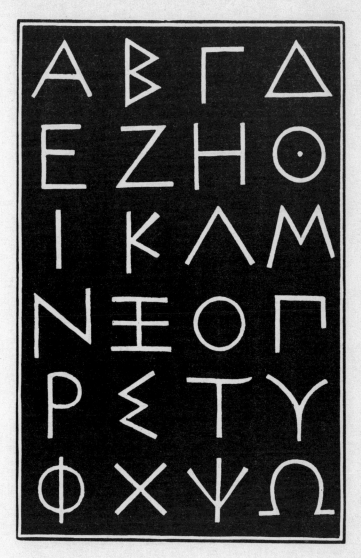

54. GREEK. FROM A STELE AT ATHENS. B.C. 394.

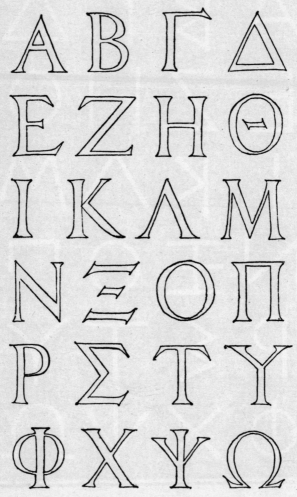

55. GREEK INITIALS, PRINTED AT BASEL. 16TH CENTURY.

ABCDE
FGHIK
LMNO
PQRST
VXYZ

56. ROMAN. FROM THE FORUM.

AABCCDE FCEFGHIL MLMLMN MNOPPPP QRRSTRR STVXVXY

57. ROMAN. FROM SCULPTURES IN THE BRITISH MUSEUM.
A.D. 150 TO 300.

AABCC
DEFGH
JLMNH
OPQRS
SSTSU

58. ANGLO-SAXON? 6TH CENTURY.

59. FROM A CODEX, 7TH OR 8TH CENTURY.

AABCD
EEFGHI
JKLMM
NOPQR
STUUV
WXYZ

60. GALICIAN MS. 8TH CENTURY.

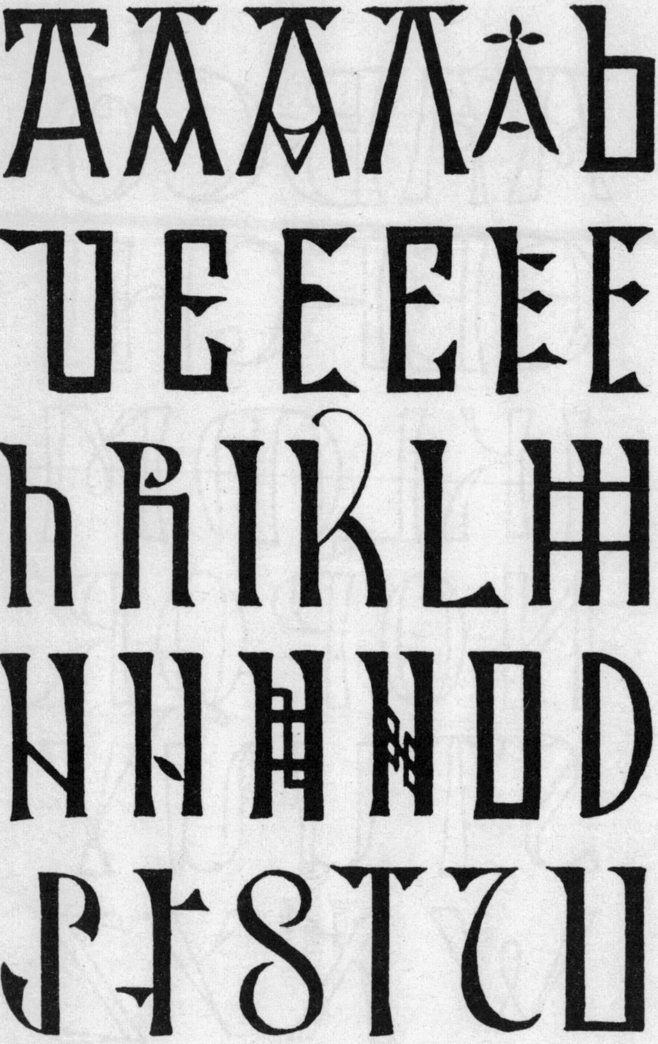

61. IRISH MS. FROM THE

BOOK OF KELLS. 8TH CENTURY.

ABCDEF

GHIJKLM

NOPQRS

TUWXYZ

62. ANGLO-SAXON MSS. 8TH AND 9TH CENTURIES.

ABCDEFG

HIKLMN

OPQRST

UVWXYZ

63. ANGLO-SAXON MSS. 8TH AND 9TH CENTURIES.

64. SAXON AND ANGLO-SAXON MSS.
7TH, 8TH, AND 9TH CENTURIES.

ABCDE
FGHIJK
LMNOP
QRSTU
VWXYZ

65. MS. 10TH CENTURY.

66. FRENCH MS. 12TH CENTURY.

AAAABB
CCⒸƆDE
EFFGGHI
LMMNNO
PRSSST
TUUVXY

67. LE PUY. WOOD. ABOUT 12TH CENTURY.

AABBC DEFGH IJKLL ΞMΝΝΟ PPQRR STTUV WXXYZ

68. 12TH CENTURY MS. GERMAN.

ABAABC
DEFFGH
IJKKJKL
MNOPQ
RSTTTU
VWXYZ

69. END OF 12TH CENTURY MSS. ENGLISH.

70. 12TH CENTURY. LISBJERG, DENMARK. GILT LETTERS ON TRANSPARENT BROWN.

ABCDE

EFGHh

ILMNO

PQRBS

TUVXZ

71. FROM A BIBLE. 13TH CENTURY.

72. FROM A GERMAN BELL. 1270.

73. FROM A PSALTER. 13TH CENTURY.

A B C D
E F G H
I K L M
N O P Q
R S T U
W X Y Z

74. MSS. 14TH CENTURY.

ABCDE
EFGHh
IJKLM
MNNOP
QRSTU
VWXYZ

75. ITALIAN. 14TH CENTURY.

76. INCISED GOTHIC CAPITALS. ABOUT 1350.

77. FROM A BRASS. NORDHAUSEN. 1397.

78. FROM A BRASS. NORDHAUSEN. 1395.

79. STONE. WESTMINSTER ABBEY. ABOUT 1400.

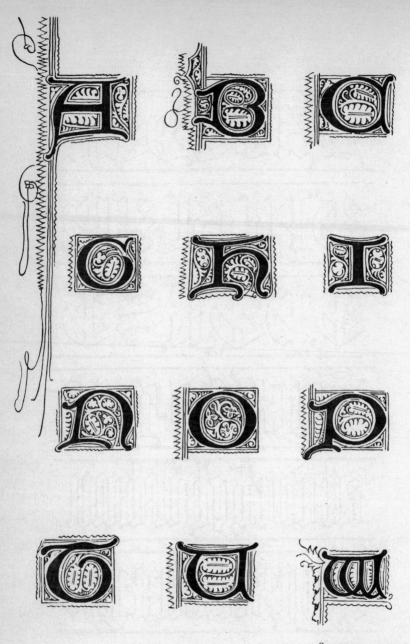

80. FROM A MS.

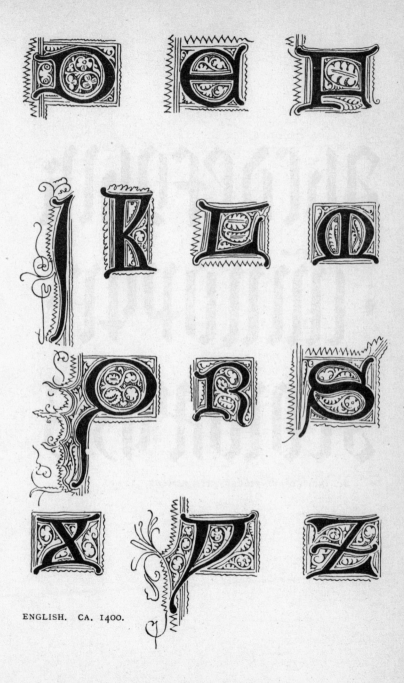

ENGLISH. CA. 1400.

abcdefghik

lṁnopqr

stvwxyzჳ

81. INCISED AND FILLED WITH CEMENT.   PRATO.   1410.

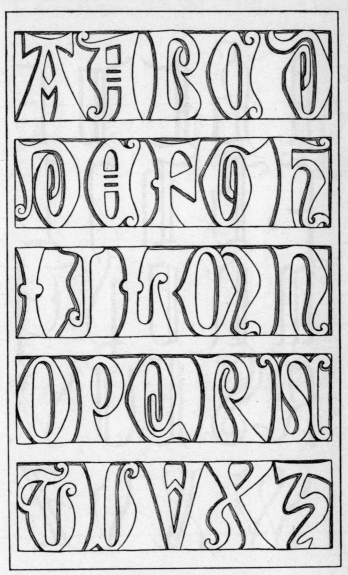

82. CARVED IN STONE.   SPANISH.

83. 1420 MS.

84. GERMAN MSS. 15TH CENTURY.

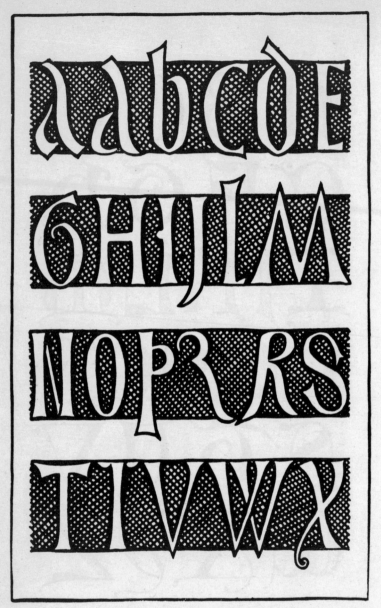

85. ENGRAVED ON BRASS. BAMBERG. 1464.

ABCDE
EEFGHI
JKLMNN
OPQRST
UVWXYZ

86. FROM A PICTURE-FRAME IN THE LOUVRE. PAINTED. 1480.

AABCOO
EFGHI
JKLM
NOPQR
SSTUV
UXYZ

87. GERMAN MSS. 1475.

88. MS. ABOUT 1475.

89. PAINTED INITIALS. CA. 1480.

90. INCISED IN MARBLE. GERMAN. 1482.

91. CARVED IN RELIEF. FRENCH. PROBABLY 15TH CENTURY.

92. INITIALS CUT IN STONE. BRUGES. CA. 1500.

abcdef

ghiklm

nopars

thwvyz

93. FROM A BRASS. END OF 15TH CENTURY.

abcdef
ghiklm
nopqst
uvwrfyz

94. FROM A BRASS. END OF 15TH CENTURY.

ABCDEEF
GHIJKLM
NOPRST
UVWXYZ
abcdefghi
klmnopqr
stuvwxyz

95. FROM MONUMENTAL INSCRIPTIONS.   END OF THE 15TH CENTURY
GERMAN.

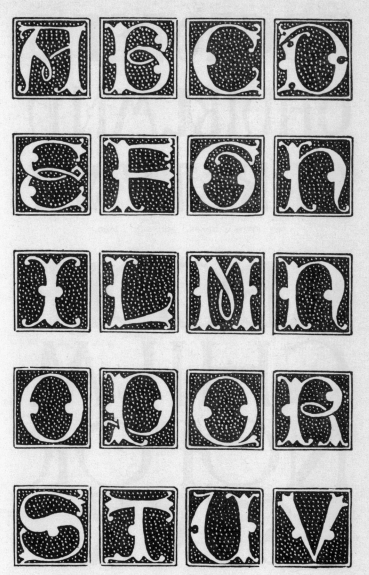

96. PRINTED INITIALS.   END OF 15TH CENTURY.

ABCLDEEFG

GHHIKLMNN

OPRSTVWZ

97. FROM A BRASS. MEISSEN. 1500.

ABCDEF

GHILM

NOPQR

STVX

98. FROM BRONZE BY PETER VISCHER. 1495.

ABCDE
FGHIKL
MNOP
QRST
VXYZ

99. INCISED. ITALIAN RENAISSANCE. S. CROCE, FLORENCE.

100. FROM A MANUSCRIPT

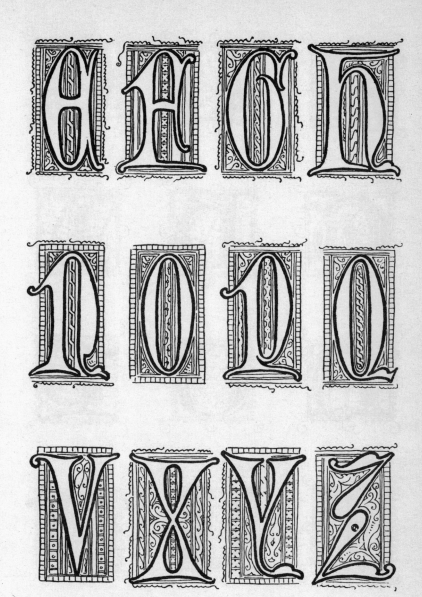

OF THE 16TH CENTURY.

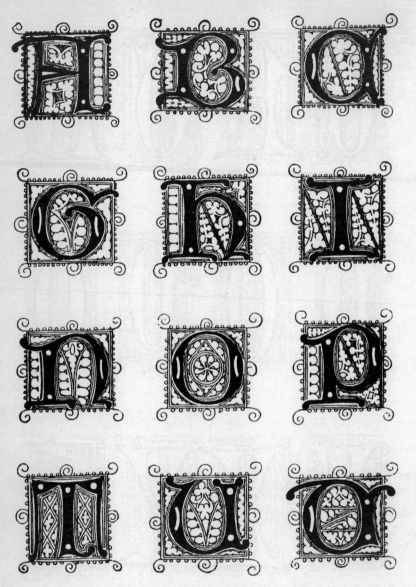

101. ITALIAN. FROM A CHORALE AT

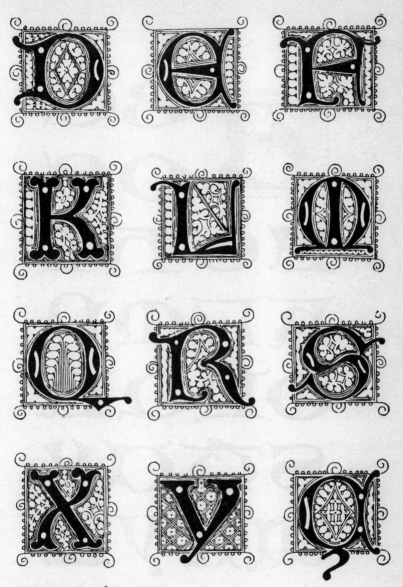

MONTE CASINO. 16TH CENTURY.

102. GOTHIC. 16TH CENTURY.

ABCDE
CFGHIL
KLMNO
PQRST
WXYZ

103. PAINTED. FLEMISH. EARLY 16TH CENTURY.

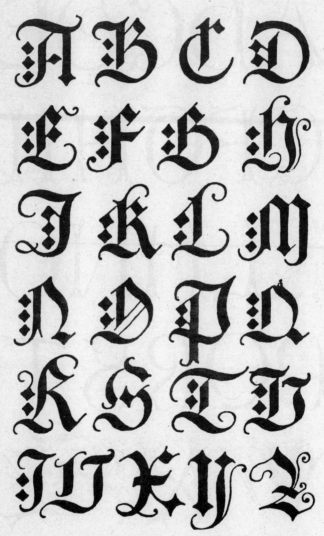

104. ALBRECHT DÜRER. EARLY 16TH CENTURY.

105. ALBRECHT DÜRER.   EARLY 16TH CENTURY.

106. ITALIAN MSS. 15TH AND 16TH CENTURIES.

107. ITALIAN. VICENTINO. 1523.

108. ITALIAN. LUDOVICO

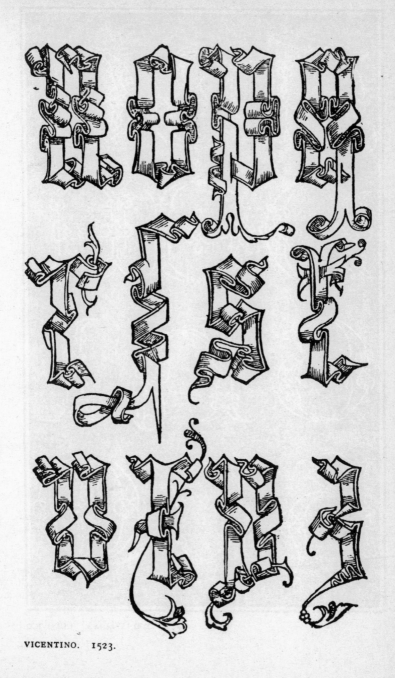

VICENTINO. 1523.

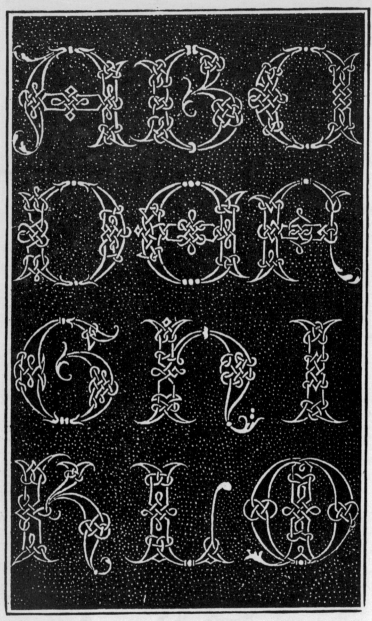

109. ITALIAN. LUDOVICO

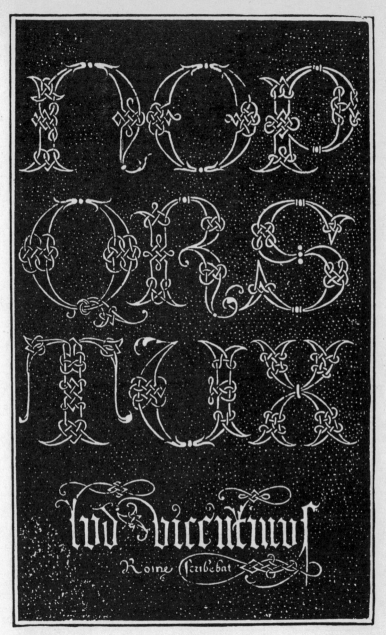

VICENTINO. 1523.

ABCDE

FGHIJ

KLMN

OPQR

STVV

WXYZ

110. AFTER LUDOVICO CURIONE. 16TH CENTURY. QY. 1530.

III. SPANISH. JUAN YCIAR. FIRST HALF OF THE 16TH CENTURY.

ABCDEFGHIJ
KLMNOPQRS
TUVVVXYZ

112. INCISED. FLORENTINE. 15TH CENTURY.

ÁAABBCC
DDEFGGH
IKKLMMN
NOPPQQR
RST VXYZ

113. ENGRAVED BY HEINRICH ALDEGREVER. CA. 1530.

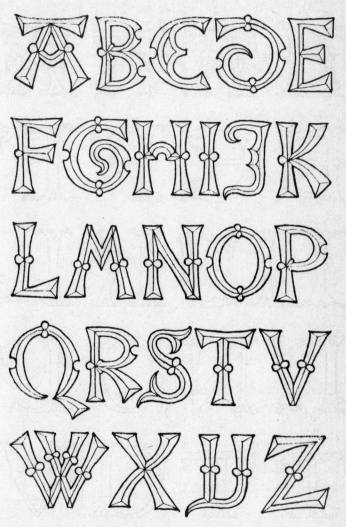

114. INCISED IN WOOD.   NORTH WALSHAM.

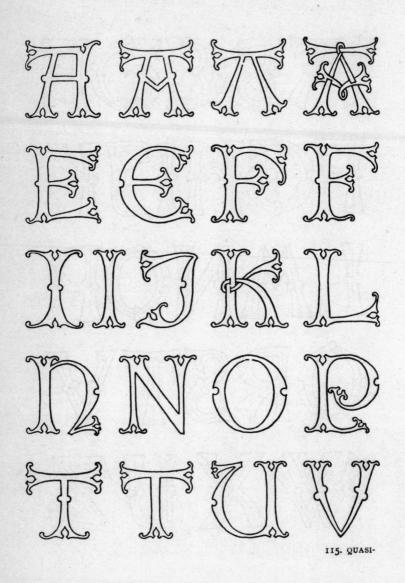

115. QUASI-

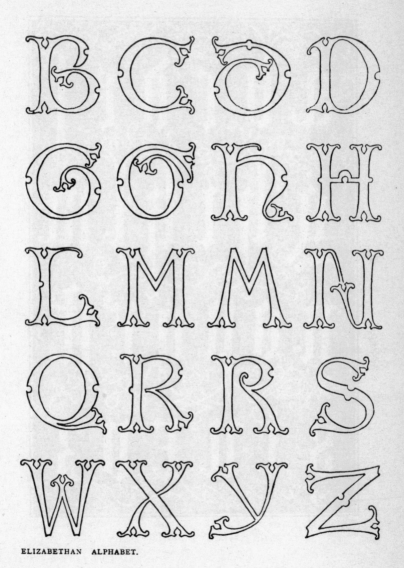

ELIZABETHAN ALPHABET.

116. ITALIAN. PALATINO. 1546.

abcdd
efgbik
lmnop
qrßfs
tuxy?

117. ITALIAN. VESPASIANO. 1556.

ABC
GHI
NOP
TVW

118. ITALIAN. SERLIO.

D E F

K L M

Q R S

X Y Z

16TH CENTURY.

119. GERMAN.

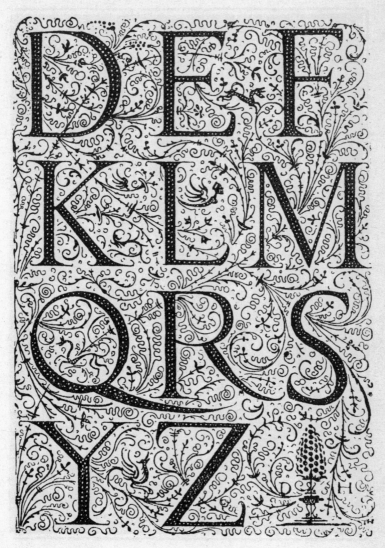

HOPFER. 1549.

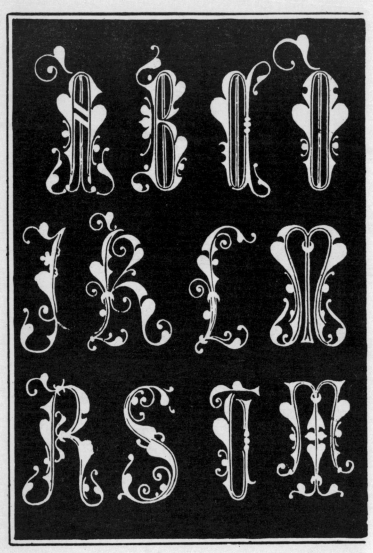

120. ITALIAN.

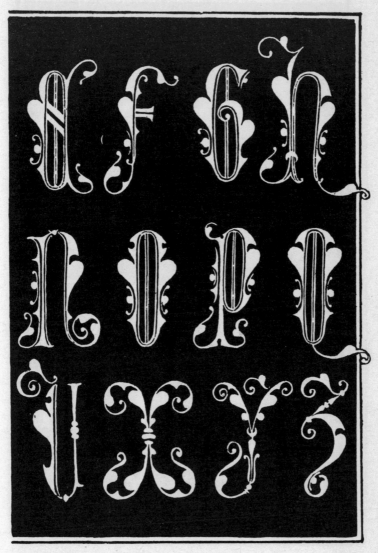

G. F. CRESCI. 1570.

121. ITALIAN. G. F. CRESCI. 1570.

Aabc
defgh
ilmno
pqrst
uxyz

122. ITALIAN. G. F. CRESCI 1570.

123. AFTER G. F. CRESCI. 1570.

abcdefghij
klmnopqr
fstuvwxyz

124. INCISED. FLEMISH. 1579.

aabbbccdeeefg
ghhijklmnnor
zsftuvvwxyz

125. INCISED. STONE. FLEMISH. 16TH CENTURY.

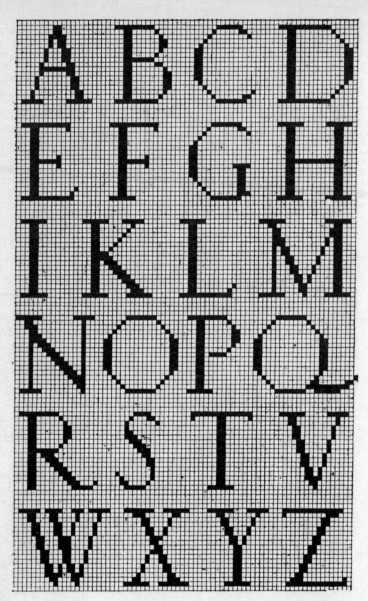

126. FROM THE LACE-BOOK OF GIOVANNI OSTAVS. 1590.

ABCDE
FGHJKL
MNOPQ
RSTUV
WXYZ

127. STONE. BINGEN. 1576, 1598, 1618.

abcde.
fghi
lmn
op qr
s tuy

128. BRASS. BAMBERG. 1613

abccde

fghijlm

mmnop

pqrrfst

stuvx

129. SLATE. WÜRZBURG. 1617.

ABCD
EFGH
IKLM
NOPQ
RSTU
WXYZ

130. PENMANSHIP. 17TH CENTURY.

abcde
fghikl
mnopq
rstuxy
z&ctæ

131. PENMANSHIP. 17TH CENTURY.

ABCD
EFGH
IJKLM
NOPQ
RSTUV
WXYZ

132. ITALICS. 17TH CENTURY.

133. CARVED IN WOOD. 1638.

$\mathcal{AABCD}$

$\mathcal{EFGH}$

$\mathcal{IKLMNO}$

$\mathcal{PQRSTV}$

$\mathcal{VWXYZ}$

$\&$

134. PENMANSHIP. E. COCKER. 1660.

Aabcdef ghiklmnopq rfstvuwxyz

135. PENMANSHIP. E. COCKER. 1660.

abcdeffghjill mnopqr₂ssat vuxyzε

136. PENMANSHIP. LESGRET. 1736.

Cocker.

A B C D E F G
H I K L M N O
P Q R S T V V W X
Y Z

et every day produce some curious Lines
That may commend thy Genius, & thy Pen.
Let all thy Vndertakings and Designes
Tend to God's Glory, and the good of men.

A a b c d e f ff g h h i k l ll m n o p p
Q q q r s s ſ s t tt ſt v u w x y y z &

137. PENMANSHIP. COCKER.

A. B. C. D. E. F. G. H.

I. K. L. M. N. O. P. Q.

R. S. T. V. W. X. y. Z

A a b c d e f g h i k l l l m n

o p g r ſ s t t t v u w x y z &

God is Alpha and Omega

138. PENMANSHIP. COCKER. 1673.

A A B C D E
F G H I K L M
N O P Q R S T V
W X Y Z

139. PENMANSHIP COCKER. 1673.

a b c d d e f g h i
j l m n o p q r s
s t u v x x y y z

140. PENMANSHIP. MAINGUENEAU. FRENCH.

Lesorel

141. PENMANSHIP. PARIS. 1736.

ABCDEFGH

IKLMNOPQ

RSTVWXY

Z. &. abcdefg

hijklmnopqrstuw

xyz AᵒDᵐ 1665.

142. STONE. WESTMINSTER ABBEY. 1665.

ABCDEFG
HIJKLMNM
NOPQQRR
STVWXYZ

abcdefghijklmn

opqrstvwxyz.

AnnoDoṁ:1697

143. INCISED. CHIPPENHAM. 1697.

abcde

fghijk

kllmno

pqrstu

vwxyz.

abcdeffg
hijkllmn
opqrſttu
vvxxyyz.

145. PENMANSHIP. C. SNELL. 1715.

Aabcdef ghilmnop grstuxz

Aabcd ef ghilmnop grstuxz̃

Aabbccddeeffg ghzbijyllmnoyp qqrzſßſtuvxxz̃z̃

146. PENMANSHIP. ANDRADE. 1721.

147. PENMANSHIP. ANDRADE. 1721.

ABCDE
FGHIJJ
KLMNO
PQRSTU
VWXYZ

148. PAINTED. GERMAN. 1727.

149. PENWORK. GERMAN. J. H. TIEMROTH. 1738-48.

abcde
efghi
klmn
opqrs
stuvx

150. STONE. OSNABRÜCK. 1742-56.

L'HOMME DISPOSE SA VOIE ET DIEU CONDUIT SES PAS

151. FRENCH. E. GUICHARD. PERIOD OF LOUIS XV.

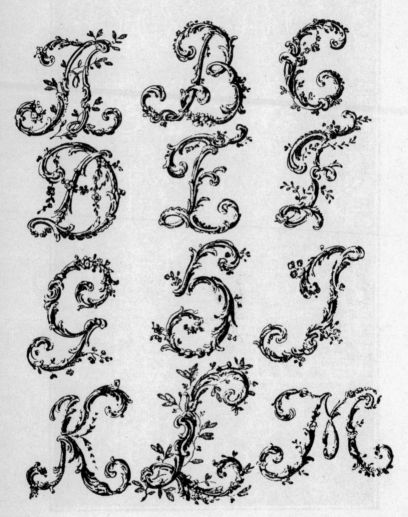

152. FRENCH. LAURENT.

PERIOD OF LOUIS XV.

abcdefghi

jklmnopqr

stuvwxyz

153. ETCHED ON LITHOGRAPHIC STONE.   NUREMBERG.
1765-70.

154. SLATE. WÜRZBURG. 1784.

ABCDEFG
HIJKLMN
OPQRSTU
VWXYZ&
12345
67890

155. PRINTED "CASLON" TYPE.

abcdefghijkl
mnopqrstuv
wxyz*ABCD*
EFGHIJKL
MNOPQRS
TUVWXYZ
abcdefghijklmn
opqrstuvwxyz

156. PRINTED "CASLON" TYPE.

157. ENGLISH COURTHAND. FROM A. WRIGHT'S "COURTHAND
RESTORED." 1815.

158. HEBREW ALPHABET.

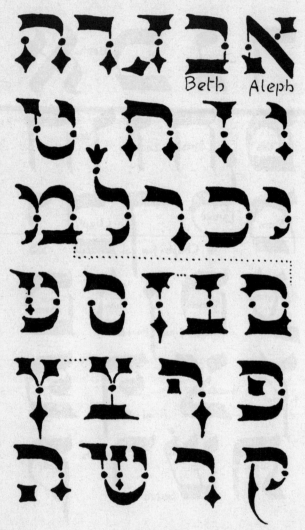

159. HEBREW ALPHABET, FROM SILVESTRE'S PALEOGRAPHIE.

MODERN ALPHABETS

SHOWING THE CHARACTER WHICH
COMES OF USING PEN, CHISEL, OR
WHATEVER IT MAY BE

A B C
G H IJ
N O P
T U V

160. PENWORK.

DEF KLM ORS XYZ

WALTER CRANE.

ABCD
EFGHIJ
KLMNO
PQRST
UWXYZ

161. PENWORK.

a b c d e f g h i j k l m n o p q r s t u v w x y z

WALTER CRANE.

162. PENWORK.

OTTO HUPP.

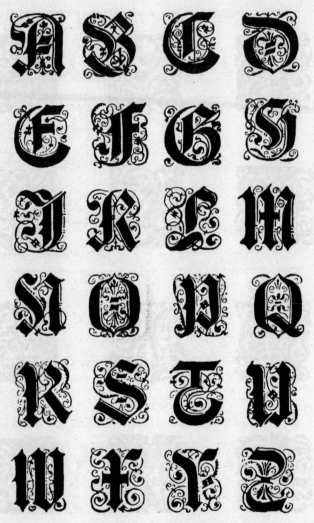

163. PENWORK. OTTO HUPP.

AAHAA
BCDOEE
FHIK K
LNOPQR
SLSTTU
VWXYZ

164. PENWORK. OTTO HUPP.

abcde
fghijk
lmnop
qrstuv
wxyz

165. PEN WRITTEN. L.F.D.

ABACD

EFGHIJ

KLKMN

OPQRS

STUVW

WXYYZ

166. PEN WRITTEN. L.F.D.

ABCDEF
GHIJKL
MNOPQ
RSTUV
WXYZ&

abcdefghij
klmnopqr
stuvwxyz

167. "OLD STYLE" ITALICS. J. VINYCOMB. PEN.

168. ITALICS. L.F.D.

ABCDEF G
HIJKLMMN
NOPQQRR
STVWXYZ

abcdefghijklmn

opqrstuvwxyz.

1234567890.

ABCDEFG
HIJKLMN
OPQRSTV
WXYZ
12345
67890

170. PENWORK. BAILEY SCOTT MURPHY, ARCHITECT.

ABCDE
FGHIKL
MNOPQ
RSTVW
XYZ &
1905

171 PENWORK. R. ANNING BELL.

172. PENWORK. R. ANNING BELL.

abcc deff
ghijklmnop
qrsßstuvwx
yz. 123 Design letters
45 into words.
67890 ABPA

173. PENWORK.   PROF. A. B. PITE, ARCHITECT.

ABCDEFG
HIJKLMNMN
OPQRSRS
TUVWXYZZ

AN ARCHITECT'S
LINE ALPHABET
FOR PENWORK.

174. PENWORK. PROF. A. B. PITE, ARCHITECT.

ABCDE
FGHIJK
LMNOP
QRSTU
VWXYZ

abcdefghijklmn
opqrstuvwxyz

175. PEN WRITTEN. B. WALDRAM.

ABCDEFG
HIJKLMN
OPQRSTU
VWXYZ&
abcdefghijk
lmnopqrstu
vwxyz & ·§·
1234567890

176. PEN WRITTEN. PERCY J. SMITH.

ABCDEF GHIJKLM NOPQRST UVWXYZ

177. PEN-DRAWN "ROMAN" CAPITALS. B. WALDRAM.

ABCDEFG HIJKLMN OPQRSTU VWXYZ &

178. PRINTED "ROMAN" TYPE. MODERN FRENCH.

ABCDGEF
GHIJKLOO
NOPQRST
UVWWXYZ

179. PEN-WRITTEN UNCIALS. B. WALDRAM.

abcdefghij
klmnopqrs
stuvwxyz

180. PEN WRITTEN. L.F.D.

ABCDEFGHI
JKLMNOPQR
STUVWXYZ
abcdefghijkl
mnopqrstuv
wxyz.

Roland Paul

181. PENWORK.   ROLAND W. PAUL, ARCHITECT.

ABCDEFGHIJ
KLMNOPQR
STUVWXYZ

182. PENWORK.   R. K. COWTAN.

ABCDEF
GHIJKLM
NOPQRST
UVWXYZ

183. PENWORK. R. K. COWTAN.

ABCDEFG
HIJKLMN
OPQRST
UVWXYZ

184. PENWORK. R. K. COWTAN.

ABCDE
EFGHIJ
KLMN
OPQR
STUVW
XYZ

185. PEN WRITTEN. WALTER WEST.

abcdefghijklmn
opqrstuvwxyz

Of course the first question is that of materi:
al; and care must be taken to choose or de:
sign an alphabet, not only practicable in,
but suitable to, the medium in which it is
to be executed. One of the commonest errors
is that of taking a style of lettering excell:
ent when written on parchment or paper, with
a quill pen, and carving it, let us say for
example, on wood. Of course the result is
often, although by no means necessarily so,
incongruous in the extreme. Many letter -
forms are, indeed, interchangeable in this
way: but if it is desired to adapt the letter.
ing of one class of object to the purposes of

186. CURSIVE WRITING. SELWYN IMAGE.

ABCDEFGHIJ KLMNOPQR STUVWXYZ

187. DESIGNED FOR ENGRAVING ON METAL; BUT NOT
UNSUITED TO PENWORK.   L.F.D.

ABCDEFGHIJ KLMNOPQR STUVWXYZ

188. PEN WRITTEN.   L.F.D.

ABCDEFG
HIJKLMN
OPQRSTU
VWXYZ &

abcdefghijkl
mnopqrstuv
wxyz

1234567890

189. FRENCH PRINTED TYPE. DESIGNED BY GRASSET (?).

ABCDEFGHIJ
KLMNOPQR
STUVWXYZ

190. ENGRAVING. ADAPTED FROM MEDIÆVAL GOLDSMITH'S WORK.
L.F.D.

ABCDEF
GHIJKLMN
OPQRST
UVWXYZ

191. L.F.D.

ABCDEFG HIJKLMN OPQRST UVWXYZ

192. L.F.D.

ABCDEFGHIJKLM NOPQRSTUVWXYZ

193. SCRATCHING. ADAPTED FROM OLD SPANISH. L.F.D.

194. INCISED. ALFRED

CARPENTER AND L.F.D.

195. WOOD.

CARVING. L.F.D.

196. ENGRAVING ON SILVER.   L.F.D.

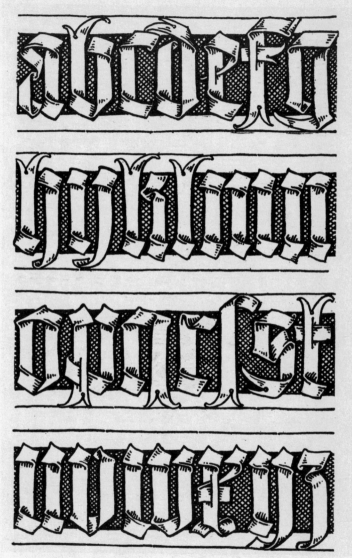

197. ENGRAVING ON BRASS. ADAPTED FROM OTTO HUPP.

198. EMBROIDERED IN COUCHED CORD.   L.F.D.

199. BEATEN METAL.   L.F.D.

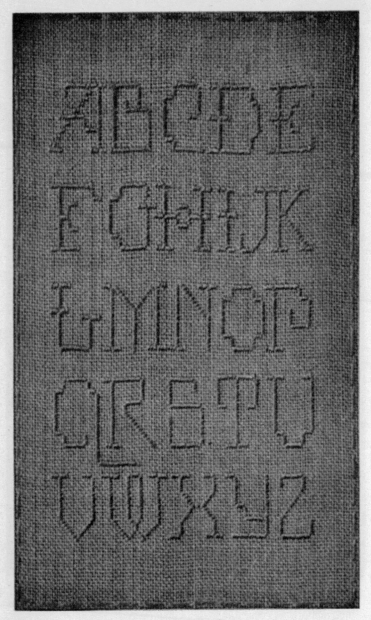

200. NEEDLEWORK. ADAPTED. L.F.D.

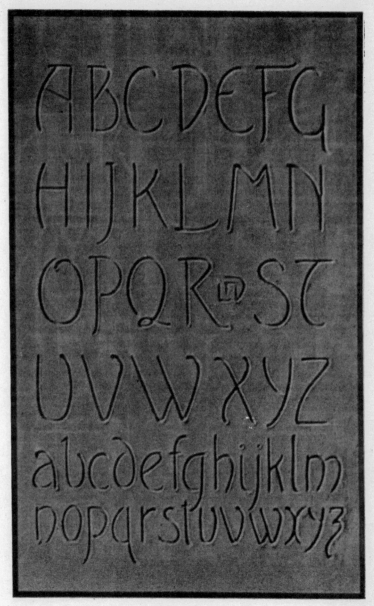

201. SGRAFFITTO. L.F.D.

202. SQUARE-CUT. QUASI-CHINESE. L.F.D.

203. BRUSHWORK. QUASI-JAPANESE. L.F.D.

ABCDEFGHI
KLMNOPQR
STUVWXYZ

abcdefghij
klmnopqrst
uvwxyz?!

204. BRUSHWORK. MUCHA.

ABCDE
FGHIJK
LMNOP
QRSTU
VWXYZ

abcdefghijklmn
opqrstuvwxyz

205. STENCILLING ADAPTED FROM E. GRASSET AND
M. P. VERNEUIL.

206. PENWORK. FRANZ STUCK.

MODERN ALPHABETS

IN WHICH THE INFLUENCE OF THE IMPLEMENT EMPLOYED IS NOT SO EVIDENT

A B C D E
F G H I J K
L M N O P
Q R S T U
V W X Y Z
a b c d e f g h i
j k l m n o p q r
s t u v w x y z

207. "SKELETON." J. VINYCOMB.

ABCDEF
GHIJKL
MNOPQR
STUVW
XYZ&&

abcdefghij
klmnopqr
stuvwxyz

208. "FRENCH." J. VINYCOMB.

ABCDE
FGHIK
LMNOP
QRSTU
VWXYZ

209. L.F.D.

ABCDE
FGHIK
LMNOP
QRSTU
VWXYZ

210. L.F.D.

ABCDEF
GHJKLM
NOPQRS
TUVWX
YZ♦1234
567890

211. J. CROMAR WATT, ARCHITECT.

ABCDEF
GHJKLM
NNOPPQ
RRSSTU
VWXYZ
abcdefghijklmn
opqrstuvwxyz. &.

212. J. W. WEEKES.

ABCDEF GHIJKLL MNOPQ RSTUV, WXYZ&

213. BLOCK CAPITALS.   W. J. PEARCE.

ABCDEF
GHIJKL
MMNOPQ
RRSSTU
VWXYYZ

abcdefghijklmn
opqrstuvwxyyzʒ.

214. "SANS SERIF."   J. W. WEEKES.

ABCDE
FGHIM
NOPQR
STUVW
XYZEK

215. GOTHIC CAPITALS.   W. J. PEARCE.

ABCD EFGHI JKLM NOPQR STUV WXYZ

216. OTTO HUPP. "ALPHABETE UND ORNAMENTE."

ABCD
IJKLM
RSTUV

217.

EFGH

NOPQ

WXYZ

L.F.D.

ABCD.
HIJKL
QRST.
XYZ.,,?
EFGHIJKL
UVWXYZ. 12

E·F·G
M·N·O·P·
U·V·W·
&· A B C D
M N O P Q R S T
3 4 5 6 7 8 9 0 ·

PATTEN WILSON.

219.

L.F.D.

ABCD

KLMN

STUV

220.

EFGHI

OPQR

WXYZ

.L.F.D.

221.

L.F.D.

ABCDEF
GHIJ KL
MNOPQR
STUVW
XYZ &

abcdefghijklm
nopqrstuvwxyz

ABCDE
FGHIJK
LMNOP
QRSTU
VWXYZ

223. MODERN GERMAN.

ABCDE
FGHIJK
LMNOP
QRSTU
VWXYZ

224. FRANZ STUCK.

AMPERZANDS AND
NUMERALS

225. AMPERZANDS. 7TH TO 15TH CENTURIES.

226. AMPERZANDS. 16TH CENTURY, ETC., FREELY RENDERED.

227. CUT IN STONE. 1477.

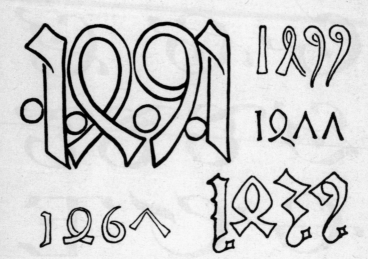

228. STONE AND BRASS. 1439-1491.

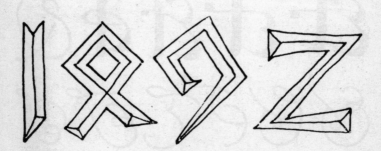

229. CUT IN STONE. 1492.

·1·5·2·0· 0·1522

15 2 0 1522

15 2 1 1522

1531 1542

15 31 1543

1533 1543 1544

1539 1545

230. CHIEFLY BRASSES. 1520–1545.

12345

12345

12345

12345

231. BRASSES.

6 7 8 9 0

6 7 8 9 0

6 7 8 9 0

6 7 8 9 0

1520–1598.

232. BRONZE. ABOUT 1550.

233. BRONZE. ABOUT 1560.

1 2 3 4 5

6 7 8 9 0

234. BRUSHWORK. FAIENCE. 16TH CENTURY.

1 2 3 4 5

6 7 8 9 0

235. BRUSHWORK. 16TH OR 17TH CENTURY.

1 2 3 4 4

6 7 8 9 0

236. ITALIAN MS. 16TH CENTURY.

1 2 3 4 5

6 7 8 9 0

237. BRUSHWORK. GILT, ON BLACK. 1548?

238. INCISED IN WOOD. GERMAN. 1588.

239. BRASS. 16TH CENTURY

1 2 3 4 5
6 7 8 9 0

240. BRUSHWORK. 16IH CENTURY.

1 2 3 4 5
6 7 8 9 0

241. ABOUT 1700.

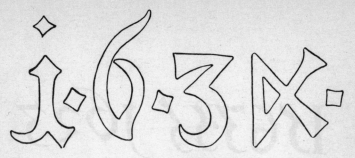

242. CUT IN STONE. 1634.

243. RELIEF IN BRASS OR BRONZE. 1647.

244. STONE. 1692.

1563·55 1623

1584 1625

1631·2 1625

1633 K679

1697 1699

1707 368

245. BRASS AND WOOD. 1563-1707.

J12334

56789

j7z6·48

J732 · 5

j744 · 9

246. 18TH CENTURY.

1716·294 1719

1727 1723

1724 1725

1735·2 1738

1755.486 1763

1774·695 1783

248. BRASS WIRE INLAY ON WOOD. 1740.

1573   1593
1649   1747

249. ENGRAVED ON STEEL, OR INLAID IN WIRE ON WOOD.
1573—1747.

250. L.F.D.

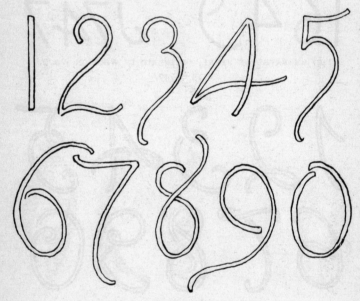

251. MODERN.

252. L.F.D.

1234567

8 9 10 11 12

253. ALÖIS MÜLLER.

12345

67890

254. L.F.D.

INDEX OF ILLUSTRATIONS
ARRANGED UNDER ARTISTS, COUNTRIES, MATERIALS & PROCESSES, AND STYLES

NOTE.—*The reference numerals are to the figure numbers of the illustrations, and in no case to pages.*